Pocket Hea

Brain Teasers, Thinking Questions,
and Non-Quantitative Questions
from Finance Job Interviews

Pocket Heard on The Street:
Brain Teasers, Thinking Questions, and Non-Quantitative Questions from Finance Job Interviews

Timothy Falcon Crack
*PhD (MIT), MCom, PGDipCom,
BSc (HONS 1st Class), IMC*

Full sized editions published 1995 (three editions). Revised 1997, 1998, 1999, 2000, 2002, 2004, 2007, 2008, 2009, 2009 (revised eBook edition), 2012, 2013 (14th Edition).

First Pocket-Sized Edition 2014.

ISBN: 978-0-9941038-2-6

Typeset by the author.
Printed in the U.S.A., U.K., and Australia.
www.InvestmentBankingJobInterviews.com
timcrack@alum.mit.edu

Contents

Preface

THIS BOOK IS A MUST READ! This pocket edition contains a careful selection of 20 brain teasers, 30 thinking questions, and over 100 non-quantitative questions collected from actual job interviews in investment banking, investment management, and options trading. The interviewers use the same questions year-after-year, and here they are. The brain teasers and more than half the thinking questions are presented with detailed solutions.

There is also a complementary pocket edition available with 75 carefully chosen quantitative questions, all with detailed solutions, taken from the same interviews (ISBN 978-0-9941-38-1-9). Those quant questions usually require a lot more math than do the brain teasers and thinking questions presented here.

The questions in these pocket editions are a careful selection taken from the full sized edition of *Heard on The Street: Quantitative Questions from Wall Street Job Interviews* (ISBN 978-0-9700552-9-3). The full sized edition is the first and the original book of quantitative questions from finance job interviews. It has been painstakingly revised over 18 years and 14 editions, and has been shaped by feedback from many hundreds of readers. With over 50,000 copies in print, its readership is unmatched by any competing book.

These questions come from all types of interviews (corporate finance, sales and trading, quant research, etc.). The questions come from all levels of interviews (undergraduate, MBA, MS, PhD). There is also a section on interview technique—based on my experiences interviewing candidates for the world's largest institutional asset manager, and also based on feedback from interviewers worldwide.

The brain teasers and thinking questions go beyond the boundaries of a typical finance education, in order to identify interviewees who have the potential to outperform their peers. That's why you need this book.

My solutions and advice are carefully designed to sharpen your skills. My advice is based on my experiences as a front line teaching assistant for MBA students at MIT, as a finance professor at Indiana University, and as the former head of a quant research team for the world's largest institutional asset manager.

My intended audience includes interviewees seeking employment at Wall Street or other finance-related firms; their interviewers, who need to weed out the hapless sheep; university professors who want to "spice up" finance courses with Wall Street job interview questions (both for fun and to show the importance of the basic concepts on The Street); students of finance who want to fill in some gaps; and finally, doctoral students in need of entertainment during periods of downtime.

I thank MIT students, MIT faculty, and practitioners. I thank Olivier Ledoit, Cecily Lown, Bingjian Ni, Eva Porro, and Juan Tenorio for their constructive criticism. The first edition of this book was written and edited in 1995 while commuting to and from MIT on the subways and buses of the Massachusetts Bay Transit Authority ("Thank you for riding... ...the MBTA").

TFC/MIT/1995

I revised this book when I was a professor at Indiana University (IU). I thank all the people thanked above (especially Olivier Ledoit). I also thank Sean Curry and The MathWorks Inc for a free copy of MATLAB (used to check answers and draw figures), MBA Style Magazine (www.mbastyle.com) for horror stories, Andres Almazan, Tom Arnold, Mary Chris Bates, Klara Buff, Alex Butler, Victor W. Goodman, Tim Hoel, Taras Klymchuk, Victor H. Lin, Marianne Lown, Alan J. Marcus, David Maslen, Marc Rakotomalala, Jason Roth, Yi Shen, Valeri Smelyansky, Dahn Tamir, Paul Turner, and students (MBA and undergraduate) at each of MIT, UCLA, and IU.

TFC/IU/1996–2000

I updated this book while working as Head of Quantitative Active Equity Research (UK/Europe) at what was the world's largest institutional asset manager. I also thank Jinpeng Chang, Mark Rubinstein, Alex Vigodner, and Nick Vivian.

TFC/London/2001–2003

I updated this book after accepting a chaired professorship in Finance at Otago University in New Zealand. I also thank Giulio Agostini, Scott Chaput, Chun Han, Alessio Farhadi, Vince Moshkevich, Katie Price, Wolfgang Prymas, Naoki Sato, Mikhail Voropaev, and also Thomas C. Watson.

This edition contains new questions and improved answers to old ones. I particularly thank interviewers at top firms who shared their most recent questions. I now also thank David Alexander, Armen Anjargholi, Arta Babaee, Edward Boyce, Veeken Chaglassian, Aidong Chen, Jun Chung, Nate Coehlo, Richard Corns, Robin Grieves, James Gwinnutt, Patrick de Man, Alexander Joura, Charles Hallion, James Hirschorn, Philip Koop, Steve Lee, Stuart O'Neill, RBP, Bryan Rasmussen, CCS, Ashish Saxena, Tommaso Sechi, Torsten Schöneborn, Adam Schwartz, Avishalom Shalit, Yirong Shen, Ian Short, Craig Smith, Olaf Torne, and Simon West.

TFC/OU/2004–2013

Two pocket editions (quant, and non-quant/brain teasers, respectively) were introduced in 2014 for several reasons: Busy readers do not always have the time to read the full sized edition; It is difficult to read the full sized edition on the subway/tube; Finally, the pocket editions are each cheaper than the full sized one.

TFC/OU/2014

Tables

Figures

Introduction

The full sized edition of this book first appeared in 1995 with questions collected from students after interviews. Nowadays the interviewers at top firms frequently send me their new questions directly! For example, one interviewer at a big-name New York investment bank sent me the bank's latest full written quantitative interview test with three dozen questions (and answers)!

I used to wonder why interviewers at top firms supply me with their interview questions to put in a book to sell to their job candidates. Now I understand that they do not mind if the questions are public knowledge because job candidates who make a serious investment of time in revising the questions deserve to be hired!

The brain teasers appear in Chapter 1, with solutions to every one in Appendix A. The thinking questions, that fall half way between brain teasers and non-quantitative questions, appear in Chapter 2, with answers, where indicated, in Appendix B. The non-quant questions appear in Chapter 3, broken into several subsections; they are not accompanied by suggested solutions. The non-quantitative questions appear here to prepare you for what you may face; your answers are in many cases going to be individual to you.

In the text, a name followed by a year (e.g., "Girsanov (1960)") refers to a work cited in the References (following the appendices).

Story: One interviewee told me that the interviewers aim to put you under as much pressure as possible, and that "you never know when they are going to bring out the guy in the chicken suit."

Questions in This Book

The questions in this book were collected by me from interviewees, interviewers, and others. I have taken the liberty of rewording them for maximum clarity because, unlike in an interview, you have no opportunity to ask me for clarification. Sometimes I give only part of a question that was asked; sometimes I combine related questions into a larger one. I remain faithful to the original problem statement wherever possible.

I sometimes add a footnote to a question. The footnote contains a slight variation on the question. Unless otherwise indicated, these "footnote questions" are made up by me and are not actual job interview questions. All other questions come from actual job interviews.

Some questions have more than one solution technique. The "right answer" may be the wrong answer if you use a "brute-force" approach and completely miss an elegant alternative.

Some questions are more difficult than others. I have labeled difficult questions with two stars "(**)." By default, all other questions deserve one star. For the more difficult questions, your approach, rather than your solution, may be of more importance. You should be able to set up a general framework for a solution. If you can solve such questions on the spot, you are doing well.

Some of the brain teasers are at a low level, and you may think it beneath your dignity to answer them. I have, however, interviewed people who claim to have degrees in finance, economics, statistics or mathematics, who cannot answer basic finance, economics, statistics, or mathematics questions, respectively. If you think the basic questions are beneath you, then prove it by walking through them like a hot knife through butter. If you cannot answer the basic questions, however, either because you are rusty on the basics, or simply never understood them, then why should anyone hire you? No one will want to put you in front of their team members, clients, or traders, who will have basic questions.

You must have already heard all the ordinary interview advice (cover letters, appearance, comments on previous employers, use of bad language, chewing gum, researching people who will interview you, researching the firm, knowing your strengths and weaknesses, and so on); if not, then see Fry (2009).

Will They Ask These Questions?

Yes; you must assume that they will. You can hope for the best, but you must prepare for the worst. Some firms use the first round of interviews to get to know you with soft and non-quantitative questions. In this case, a second round typically follows with quantitative questions or brain teasers. Other firms use a quantitative first round to screen applicants up front. However, some firms ask no quantitative questions or brain teasers. There is thus a chance that you will see none of those.

Other Advice

I cannot stress highly enough that you are not just interviewing for the job that was advertised. There are other openings in the firm that have not yet been advertised (and may never be advertised), and there are openings in other firms that your interviewer knows about because he or she knows people there. There will also be other openings at the interviewing firm in the future. If they like you and your CV, but do not think you are suited to that one job, they may recommend you strongly to another team leader within their firm or even at another firm. The implication of this is that if you discover quickly that you are not suited to the position advertised, or the firm, then you should steer the interview toward your strengths and ask the interviewer to keep you in mind for other positions. He or she may even tell you of another opening.

This works in reverse also. If your interview is awful, the interviewer will happily pass that information to other people who ask about you, or even without being asked if you really stink.

The finance community is small and interwoven and corporate memory is long. If you interviewed at the firm before, your interviewer probably knows about it and will talk to the people you talked to, even if they have moved on. Indeed, if you worked/interviewed/studied anywhere in the world, the interviewer can find a former colleague, interviewer, adviser etc, of yours, who is known to them and who can assess you. Your resume may have circulated widely within the firm, both in its local offices and overseas, before you set foot in the building or pick up the phone. Indeed, your resume might have circulated so widely that no one informs HR, and no one even remembers where your resume came from; that can explain why you never got any response, not even a rejection.

Your resume is a starting point. Do not inflate it. You *will* be asked about it. When a resume arrives on the desk of the interviewer, he or she looks at it and tries to figure out in advance some questions to ask. If you write on your resume that you took an option pricing class, and got an "A," then if the interviewer is an option pricing nut, you just guaranteed that the interview is going to get hot. If the area is a weakness for you, then do not make yourself a target. If you want to advertise that you took the class, then that is fine, but prepare yourself for incoming questions. Let me add that on 100% of CVs where the candidate lists "attention to detail" as a skill, I have found obvious errors caused by a lack of attention to detail. Get your resume proofread by people for whom English is their first language.

I received three cover letters that stand out in my mind. One from a young woman applying for a junior quant position who stated that she had "a lot of love to give," one from a graduate of Rutgers who seemed to think I was sufficiently stupid not to have heard of Rutgers and felt the need to describe the school in great detail, and one from someone saying that they had always wanted to work in investment banking (when I was working at that time for an asset management company). Remember that you have sent your CV and cover letter out to act as your ambassador in your absence! A substandard effort here can kill your opportunity for an interview as surely as any ridiculous social media Web page can.

Do not smoke just before your interview. Get a stop smoking patch or something similar. The same goes for garlic for 24 hours before your interview. It stinks! Similarly, no one likes shaking hands with a limp dead fish. If your hands drip like a leaky faucet, then put your hand in your pocket (warm and dry), or palm down on your lap right up until you get up to shake hands. It is simple but effective.

One out of every three men I have ever interviewed put their finger up their nose during the interview. I kid you not. They seem to be unaware of it. Perhaps it is nerves. They expect me to shake hands with them at the end of the interview, but I always find a way out of it. Keep your damn hands off your face during the interview!

Intelligent or genuinely humorous small talk is fine, but do not make a fool of yourself. For example, one guy came back a week later for a second round interview with me. I went to greet him in the foyer, and he looked at me blankly. Then he suddenly said "I remember you!" and "This is for the quant position, right?" Those were his first words!

Cover letters go in the garbage can, and e-mails are deleted. Make sure your e-mail address and phone number are on your resume. Similarly, buy an answering machine (or get reliable voice mail) and check it often. If HR cannot find you quickly, then someone else can interview for your job before you.

Do not ask how many hours they work, or what they pay. You do not care how many hours it takes; You love working long days and nights. You do not care what the pay is; you just want to get your foot in the door.

Show passion. The words "I want this job" should come out of your mouth plainly and clearly during the interview. Why do I say that? Well, surprisingly often, when the job candidate has gone, we ask ourselves whether he/she really wanted the job, and we conclude that they did not. Sometimes we are surprised to subsequently hear from some mutual contacts that the candidate was shattered not to get to the next stage. Hell, you acted like you did not want the job! Show some passion; make it plain.

Show that you love the industry and the challenge. Even if the market is bad, and you are out of work, you must be upbeat. If you tell me a tale of woe, all I can think is that "99% of your life is what you make it, and if your life sucks, you suck." Why would I want you sitting next to me at work all day? Be positive. People like people who like them.

Finally, the ex-post probability that you get the job is either zero or one. If you prepare as though it is zero, then it will be. If you prepare as though it can be one, then you can make it so.

Please feel free to send me e-mails with queries, corrections, alternative solutions, but especially with new interview questions. The errata (with corrections and comments) can be found at the website below.

www.InvestmentBankingJobInterviews.com
timcrack@alum.mit.edu

Chapter 1

Brain Teasers

The only prerequisites for answering the questions in this chapter are elementary quantitative skills and common sense. Many questions in this chapter have two solution techniques: an elegant technique requiring little or no computation and a "hammer-and-tongs" brute-force approach. The technique you choose is revealing. Solutions for question in this chapter are in Appendix A.

Q 1.1: You are given two glass jugs. Each contains the same volume, V, of liquid. One jug contains pure alcohol, and the other jug contains pure water. A modest quantity, Q, of water is poured from the water jug into the alcohol jug, which is then thoroughly mixed. The same modest quantity, Q, of (now diluted) alcohol is then poured back into the water jug to equalize the volumes of the jugs at their initial levels.

The initial concentration of alcohol in the alcohol jug equals the initial concentration of water in the water jug (at 100%). What is the relationship between the final concentrations of alcohol in the alcohol jug and water in the water jug?[1]

Q 1.2: Your bedroom sock drawer contains eight red socks and 11 blue socks that are otherwise identical. The light is broken in your bedroom, and you must select your socks in the dark. What is the minimum number of socks you need to take out of your drawer and carry into your (well-lit) living room to guarantee that you have with you at least a matching pair to choose from?

Q 1.3: I have dropped 10,000 ants randomly onto a ruler that is one meter (i.e., 100 centimeters) long and oriented to point north–south. The ants are of very small size and mass. Each ant walks at a steady pace of one centimeter per second in a straight line parallel to the long edge of the ruler. Their initial direction is randomly either north or south. The ants are all from the same colony and possess an inherited vision problem: they have peripheral vision only. This means that they can collide with each other if they meet head on (although very small, they are large enough to collide). If two ants do collide head on, however, then they each turn around instantly and head back the

---

[1]This is not a chemistry problem. Please ignore the fact that mixing a volume V_1 of water with a volume V_2 of alcohol results in a total volume less than $V_1 + V_2$.

way they came at their steady pace. With so many ants in one small space, a single ant may experience multiple collisions before it walks off of the ruler. So, how long must you wait to be sure that all the ants have walked off of the ruler?

Q 1.4: (*) A windowless room contains three identical light fixtures, each containing an identical light bulb. Each light fixture is connected to one of three switches outside of the room. Each bulb is switched off at present. You are outside the room, and the door is closed. You may flip any of the external switches in any manner you choose. After this, you must take your hands off the switches and then you may go into the room and do as you please (but you will not be allowed to damage anything or touch the switches again). How can you tell which switch goes to which light?

Q 1.5: A small boat is floating in a swimming pool. The boat contains a very small but very heavy rock. If the rock is tossed out of the boat into the pool, what happens to the water level in the pool?

Q 1.6: I have a 20 × 20 chessboard and a very large box of identical cubes. Each square on the chessboard is the same size as the face of any cube. I am going to arrange piles of cubes on the chessboard in a special pattern. I align one edge of the board so it is running north–south. I start at the northwest corner by placing one cube on that square. Whenever I step to the south or the east, I place a pile of cubes containing one more cube than in the previous square. This produces the pattern in Figure 1.1. How many cubes in total are there on the chessboard?

1	2	3	4	$\cdots$	19	20
2	3	4	5	$\cdots$	20	21
3	4	5	6	$\cdots$	21	22
4	5	6	7	$\cdots$	22	23
$\vdots$	$\vdots$	$\vdots$	$\vdots$	$\ddots$	$\vdots$	$\vdots$
19	20	21	22	$\cdots$	37	38
20	21	22	23	$\cdots$	38	39

Figure 1.1: Number of Cubes on Each Square of a 20×20 Chessboard (Q)

Q 1.7: You have a chessboard (8×8) plus a big box of dominoes (each 2×1). I use a marker pen to put an "X" in the squares at coordinates (1,1) and (8,8)—a pair of diagonally opposing corners. Is it possible to cover the remaining 62 squares using the dominoes without any of them sticking out over the edge of the board and without any of them overlapping? You must not damage the board or the dominoes in the process or do anything weird like standing them on their ends—just answer the question.[2]

---

[2]Naoki Sato has suggested a follow up question. Place an "X" on two squares: one black, and one white. Can you cover the remaining squares with dominoes? See Answer 1.7 for the solution.

Q 1.8: You have a string-like fuse that burns in exactly one minute. The fuse is inhomogeneous, and it may burn slowly at first, then quickly, then slowly, and so on. You have a match, and no watch. How do you measure exactly 30 seconds?

Q 1.9: You have two string-like fuses. Each burns in exactly one minute. The fuses are inhomogeneous, and may burn slowly at first, then quickly, then slowly, and so on. You have a match, and no watch. How do you measure exactly 45 seconds?

Q 1.10: How many places are there on the Earth where you can walk one mile south, one mile east, one mile north, and end up exactly where you started? Assume the Earth is a perfect sphere, that your compass bearing is constant on each leg of the walk, that all parts of the Earth are able to be walked upon, and that your feet are arbitrarily small.

Q 1.11: This is an absolute classic. A king demands a tax of 1,000 gold sovereigns from each of 10 regions of his nation. The tax collectors for each region bring him the requested bag of gold coins at year end. An informant tells the king that one tax collector is cheating and giving coins that are consistently 10% lighter than they should be, but he does not know which collector is cheating. The king knows that each coin should weigh exactly one ounce. How can the king identify the cheat by using a weighing device exactly once?

Q 1.12: Again, an absolute classic. You hire a man to work in your yard for seven days. You wish to pay him in gold. You have one gold bar with seven parts—like a chocolate bar. You wish to pay him one gold part per day, but you may snap the bar in only two places. Where do you snap the bar so that you may pay him at the end of each day, and so that on successive days he may use what you paid him previously to make change?

Q 1.13: Why are images in a mirror flipped horizontally and not vertically? For example, although I wear my wristwatch on my left wrist, and my reflection wears his on his right wrist, my reflection is not standing on his head.

Q 1.14: (**) I am told this is a genuine finance interview question. It had to be a trading interview, because no one but a trader would ask this in an interview. I considered transforming the question, but left it as is for authenticity. Avert your eyes if you are easily offended!

How can three men and one women have mutually safe heterosexual intercourse with just two condoms? Assume that no condom can break or leak, and that you cannot wash a used one.[3]

---

[3]With one man and three women, the answer is of similar type, but different. This question also appears in Derman (2004, p104), which is probably how it drifted to Wall Street.

Q 1.15: Can the mean of two consecutive prime numbers ever be prime?

Q 1.16: A pizza question! You order a pizza for six people. The diameter of the pizza is 12 inches. What would the diameter have to be to feed eight people? Yes, this is a derivatives question.

Q 1.17: Consider the following game: a player tosses a fair coin until a head appears; if the head occurs on the kth toss, the player gets a payoff of $\$2^k$, and the game ends.[4]

1. What is the fair value of the game? That is, what is the expected payoff to a player?

2. A very important customer is on the line and wants you to quote him a bid-ask spread for exactly one play of the game. "Hurry up, I haven't got all day!" You have 15 seconds.

Q 1.18: I am going to toss four coins. You are going to toss five coins. You win if you get strictly more heads than I do. What is the probability that you win?

Q 1.19: (**) Two sealed envelopes are handed out. You get one and your competitor gets the other. You

---

[4]This game is over 250 years old and is known as the "St. Petersburg Game." It is quoted by Daniel Bernoulli (Latin version, 1738; English translation, 1954).

understand that one envelope contains m dollars, and the other contains $2m$ dollars (where m is unstated).[5]

1. If you peek into your envelope, you see $X. However, you do not know whether your opponent has $2X$ or $\frac{1}{2}X$. *Without peeking*, what is your expected benefit to switching envelopes? What is your opponent's expected benefit to switching envelopes (assuming your opponent sees $Y)? Should you switch? If you do switch, should you do it again for exactly the same reason (assuming neither of you peeked)?

2. Suppose that you both peek into your envelopes initially. What is the payoff to switching? Should you switch? If you do, do you do it again for the same reason?

Q 1.20: Four cards are shuffled and placed face down in front of you. Their faces (hidden) display the four elements: water, earth, wind, and fire. You are to turn the cards over one at a time until you either win or lose. You win if you turn over water and earth. You lose if you turn over fire. What is the probability that you win?

---

[5]This problem is over 40 years old and is known as the "Exchange Paradox."

Chapter 2

Thinking Questions

These thinking questions lie between brain teasers and non-quantitative questions. Many of these questions have some sort of precise solution. However, if you know exactly how many McDonalds' outlets there are in the US and say so directly, then you have missed the point. The interviewer wants you to work the answer out and describe your reasoning <u>out loud</u>. An **(A)** indicates that the answer appears in Appendix B

Q 2.1: **(A)** How many McDonald's fast food outlets are there in the US?

Q 2.2: **(A)** You are in a jail cell alone stripped of your possessions. It is Friday afternoon, and you desperately need a cigarette. How do you force the guard to give you one?

Q 2.3: **(A)** I toss a coin 100 times and get 100 heads in a row. What is the probability that the next outcome will be a head?

Q 2.4: **(A)** How do you weigh a jet aeroplane without using scales?

Q 2.5: **(A)** Explain why aeroplanes can fly.

Q 2.6: **(A)** What do you think of our tombstone in today's *Wall Street Journal*?

Q 2.7: **(A)** With your abilities, you seem to not fit in this position (or this firm). Perhaps you should consider a job in ...

Q 2.8: **(A)** Tell me 10 things you can use a pencil for, other than for writing.

Q 2.9: **(A)** Do you believe that markets are efficient?

Q 2.10: **(A)** What are the "Dow Jones Dogs"?

Q 2.11: **(A)** When inflationary fears arise, the government has two forms of macroeconomic policy to try to slow the economy down. Name these and explain them in a few words.

Q 2.12: **(A)** When is a motor vehicle that is owned by the company not recorded on the balance sheet as PPE ("physical plant and equipment" or "property plant and equipment")?

Q 2.13:   (**A**) How many quarters would you need to stack on top of each other to reach the top of the Empire State Building?

Q 2.14:   (**A**) In the calculation of free cash flow, does the level of long-term debt matter?

Q 2.15:   (**A**) Why do beer cans have tapered tops and bottoms?

Q 2.16:   (**A**) What is $\sqrt{204,000}$?

Q 2.17:   (**A**) Why are manhole covers round?

Q 2.18:   If a cannonball is dropped in the deepest part of the Earth's oceans, how long will it take to reach the ocean floor?

Q 2.19:   If a coin is dropped from the top of the Empire State Building, how long until it hits the sidewalk?

Q 2.20:   How many gas stations are there in the US?

Q 2.21:   How many elevators (i.e., "lifts" if you are British) are there in the US?

Q 2.22:   How would you value an option on (famous basketball player) Michael Jordan?

Q 2.23:   How many ping-pong balls can you fit in a jumbo jet (e.g., Boeing 747)?

Q 2.24:   How would you move Mount Fuji?

Q 2.25: If you were a color (animal, famous person, ...) which one would you be, and why?

Q 2.26: You have a five-gallon jar and a three-gallon jar. You can have as much water as you want. How do you put exactly four gallons into the five-gallon container? This is too easy for me to supply an answer.

Q 2.27: Estimate the annual demand for car batteries.

Q 2.28: What would you estimate to be the size of the racquetball market in the US?

Q 2.29: You are to build a plant for Coors to serve all beer customers in the state of Ohio. How large would you build it? That is, specifically how many cans (of the new wide-mouth variety) do you anticipate being demanded for the year?

Q 2.30: How many fish are there in the Earth's oceans?

Q 2.31: How many barbers are there in Chicago?

> **Story:** One of my students who got a job at a large mutual fund company described his firm's working environment as follows: "Dig a hole, fill the hole with water, fill the water with sharks, and promote anything that crawls out alive."

Chapter 3

Non-Quantitative Questions

I am a quant. I hate invasive, wishy-washy, touchy-feely, namby-pamby, non-quantitative interview questions, that I cannot solve using math. If you have prepared for the quantitative questions (using one of my other books), and for the brain teasers, but you are dreading those wishy-washy, non-quantitative questions, then you need to read this chapter.[1]

---

[1] As mentioned in the introduction, you can buy interview books containing general non-quantitative questions. However, these books do not cover finance-related non-quantitative questions or the quirky questions unique to investment banking interviews. Of these interview books, I recommend Fry (2009). He presents non-quantitative questions and weighs up good and bad responses.

Some of these questions have a single correct answer (great!). Others are roughly what you might expect in some sort of Freudian couch session after having been arrested for machine-gunning all the bag boys in your local supermarket. Some of the questions depend upon knowledge of financial management; others depend upon how many drinks you had at that last party you went to (and you might not get the job if you did not have any drinks at the last party or if you do not go to parties).

Speaking of parties, I saw some guy turn up to an interview without a tie, and another turned up wearing white shoes. You are not expected to own a $5,000 suit, but you are expected to look sensible, not like you are going to a retro 1970's party.

I have three pieces of general advice about answering non-quantitative questions. First, be honest. There is no point in manufacturing some false response to help you get a job at a place where you do not fit and will not ever be happy. How long is a job like that going to last, and what sort of an impression will you leave behind? Second, just because you are being honest does not mean you have to reveal all. Think about the interviewer's goals. They want to know whether you can do the job, and whether you fit. When they ask you about yourself, give them enough information to figure out whether you can do the job and whether you fit, but do not go too far beyond that. I have many times had job candidates supply some quirky tidbit of information about themselves that they thought was interesting or entertaining, when, in fact, it was boring or quite damning. Third, practice your answers with a friend who is also job hunting. Take turns being the interviewer and then tell each other when a response raised a flag.

Some candidates like to say "um," or (much worse) "like," over and over. After you have said "like" ten times, your interviewer (who looks like he or she is really concentrating, and hanging on your every word) may actually have switched off completely, and started counting how many times you say "like." After the interview they can return to the office and report the count back to their colleagues. Like totally dude! If this is you, then practice being interviewed by a friend who whacks you on the leg with a ruler every time you say the offending word, until you stop.

My non-quantitative questions are broken into four categories: questions about you, questions about your job awareness, questions about the markets or the economy, and questions about financial management.

This chapter benefited very much from interview questions collected by second-year MBA students at MIT's Sloan School of Management and MBA students at Indiana University. I also thank many interviewers at investment banks for sharing their questions with me.

Story: A student of mine interviewing at a top bulge bracket firm was asked to draw a picture of himself! They gave him pencil and paper, and he drew a picture (into his picture he also drew books, friends, and other goofy stuff to indicate that he was not retarded).

You

Q 3.1: Why are you here today?

Q 3.2: Tell me about yourself.

Q 3.3: Walk me through your resume.

Q 3.4: What are your career goals? How will you achieve those goals?

Q 3.5: What do you see yourself doing in five years? Is this different from what you imagined when you entered the degree program at your college (if so, how so)?

Q 3.6: Describe your life experiences, explaining any major decisions you have made to date.

Q 3.7: What two or three accomplishments have given you particular satisfaction over your lifetime?

Q 3.8: Tell me in detail what you did while working for this company (that appears on your resume).

Q 3.9: How would you value yourself in financial terms?

Q 3.10: How do you evaluate your success or the success of others?

Q 3.11: How would you describe yourself? How would your friends describe you? How would a former supervisor describe you?

Q 3.12:   What is your greatest strength?

Q 3.13:   Describe a situation where you successfully sold your ideas.

Q 3.14:   What is your greatest weakness?

Q 3.15:   What areas of your performance need improvement?

Q 3.16:   Describe the type of work environment in which you would, or conversely would not, excel.

Q 3.17:   Why shouldn't we hire you? ...a tough spin on the traditional "what is your greatest weakness" question.

Q 3.18:   Tell me something you tried but ended up quitting on.

Q 3.19:   What is the biggest risk you have taken in your life?

Q 3.20:   Rate yourself on a scale of 1 to 10 on the type of risk taker you are. Tell me why and give examples to support your claims.

Q 3.21:   Tell me about a goal you set for yourself in the past that turned out to be either too easy or too hard to achieve. What did you learn from the situation?

Q 3.22:   What distinguishes you from other candidates we might hire?

Q 3.23: What do you do for fun?

Q 3.24: Describe the best party you have ever been to.

Q 3.25: What is the biggest investment mistake you have ever made?

Q 3.26: Tell me about a time when you had to deal with a highly ambiguous situation. What did you do? How did you deal with it?

Q 3.27: Please describe an ethical dilemma you have faced at work, and tell me how you handled the situation.

Q 3.28: How good are your writing skills? Please give me some convincing evidence.

Q 3.29: If you could go on a cross-country car trip with any three people, who would you choose?

Q 3.30: If you were holding a dinner party, and you could invite any three dead people (presumably resurrected), who would you choose? Please do not choose any relatives.

Q 3.31: Why did you decide to apply to your MBA college? Did you apply to other MBA programs (if so, which ones and why)?

Q 3.32: What do you do if the "picture-in-picture" does not work on your television? Yes, one of my students was asked this in a banking interview!

Q 3.33: How would you evaluate your experiences at your MBA college?

Q 3.34: What are the strengths and weaknesses of your MBA program?

Q 3.35: Describe a situation in which you had to make a decision based on very little information.

Q 3.36: Tell me about a situation when you were chosen as a leader by the members of your group.

Q 3.37: Repeat the conversation that you had with your team mates when things did not go well in your group.

Q 3.38: What have you enjoyed most about your experiences at your MBA college? What would you change?

Q 3.39: What is your GPA at your college? What about your GMAT score?

Q 3.40: Which courses did you enjoy most at your MBA college (and why)?

Q 3.41: How has your course work at your MBA college helped you to develop skills relevant to this job?

Q 3.42: What has been most difficult for you at your MBA college, and how have you dealt with it?

Q 3.43: How much of your education did you personally fund?

Q 3.44:   How do you spend your time outside of school and work? How do you balance your life?

Q 3.45:   Describe your typical day.

Q 3.46:   Are you innately intelligent, or do you have to work really hard?

Q 3.47:   At interview end: "Is there anything important you have not had a chance to tell me?"

Q 3.48:   At interview end: "Do you have any questions you would like to ask me?" You must have questions; Candidates with no questions appear unmotivated/uninterested. Saying no is like slapping your interviewer in the face. That is no way to end the interview! Your questions must be ones whose answers cannot be found easily online. For example, "What is the biggest challenge facing your division over the next two years?," "Why did you join the company?," "What do you personally find most satisfying about working for this company?"

Your Job Awareness

Q 3.49:   What do you know about us? What makes us different that appeals to you?

Q 3.50:   How does this position in this company fit into your career development plans? What other career options are you considering?

Q 3.51: Why do you want to work for this employer?

Q 3.52: Sell yourself to me. Prove to me that you are someone I should seriously consider for our firm.

Q 3.53: What motivates you to put forth your best effort? What type of work environment brings out your best effort?

Q 3.54: What rewards do you seek from work? What rewards do you seek from this particular job (or company)?

Q 3.55: Tell me about a recent deal our company did. Walk me through the details of the deal.

Q 3.56: Why are you not better matched with Firm X (our competitor)?

Q 3.57: Do you have any geographical preferences? What are your thoughts about travel or relocation?

Q 3.58: What do you see yourself contributing to our organization, both in the short term and in the long term?

Q 3.59: What other companies are you interviewing with, and how do we compare?

Q 3.60: Why fixed income rather than equities?

Q 3.61: What do you think it takes to be successful in this position (or this organization)?

Q 3.62: Why do you want to work as a trader?

Q 3.63: What do you think traders do?

Q 3.64: If you were in my position, interviewing candidates for this position, what qualities would you seek? How would you evaluate candidates?

Q 3.65: Describe the best boss you have ever had. How would you define the qualities of a good manager?

Q 3.66: What do you think an investment banker does?

Q 3.67: Do you understand the hours investment bankers work and why?

Q 3.68: Describe how you build relationships in a new job.

Q 3.69: Imagine you have received three job offers. How will you decide which one to accept?

Q 3.70: If you were to get two other job offers in addition to one from us, from which firms would they most likely come, would you take them, and why?

Q 3.71: Some people say investment banking is not value adding. How do you refute that?

Q 3.72: Imagine you are giving a presentation to a client and they tell you your numbers are wrong. What would you do?

Q 3.73:   If we offer you a job right now, will you take it?

Markets or the Economy

Q 3.74:   Where is the DOW, or S&P500, or NIKKEI, or FTSE, or Hang Seng, or....? How does it compare now to where it has been over the last two years? Where do you see it two weeks from now (or six months from now)?

Q 3.75:   Where is the JPY, or GBP, or CAD, or EUR, or....? How does it compare now to where it has been over the last two years? Where do you see it two weeks from now (or six months from now)?

Q 3.76:   What does Company X (a well known company) actually do?

Q 3.77:   Do you trade? Do you own stock? What made you choose those stocks?

Q 3.78:   What would you do if I gave you $10,000 to trade with? (Note that if you have never opened a brokerage account, you must not give lack of funds as an excuse. If you cannot generate $2,000 to open a brokerage account, then why should I hire you?)

Q 3.79: What is LIBOR, and what is today's LIBOR rate?[2]

Q 3.80: Why invest in a particular market (e.g., Korea, Russia, Germany)?

Q 3.81: Tell me how you keep up with the news.

Q 3.82: Talk me through a transaction/event/deal in the finance industry that caught your eye recently. What is a problem with this deal? What's another problem? What's another problem? Why is this a problem? (They may push and push until you cannot go any further or until you get to the problem they want you to identify).

Q 3.83: How would the following affect interest rates: A relative of Saddam Hussein starts making trouble in the Middle East; there is another Asian currency crisis; Monica Lewinsky (alleged mistress of the US president Clinton) hits the headlines again as the alleged mistress of the current US president.

Q 3.84: What stock do you recommend and why?

---

[2]They probably mean the benchmark three- or six-month US dollar LIBOR rates, but they might not say that. There are several different dimensions here: you should understand the distinction between USD LIBOR and GBP LIBOR, between three-month USD LIBOR and six-month USD LIBOR, between LIBOR (London InterBank Offered Rate) and EURIBOR (Euro Interbank Offered Rate), and between euro LIBOR and EURIBOR. If you do not, look in your favorite investments book, or use a Web search engine.

Q 3.85:   What sector should I be short? What sector should I be long?

Q 3.86:   Tell me about a stock you like or hate and why.

Q 3.87:   What should be the (CAPM) beta for Intel Corp.?

Q 3.88:   Where do you think the US economy will go over the next year?

Q 3.89:   Tell me how the Dow Jones Industrial Average is calculated.

Q 3.90:   Draw the yield curve showing 3M, 6M, 1YR, 2YR, 5YR, 10YR, 30YR rates.

Q 3.91:   Do you think the stock market is efficient (in an EMH sense)? A very popular question for asset management.

Q 3.92:   Suppose you are actively investing to beat the market. Are there more opportunities (i.e., inefficiencies) in the S&P500 or in the 500 largest stocks in Europe?

Q 3.93:   What is a black swan? What do black swans mean for the use of VaR and other conventional statistical methods employed in quantitative finance? This obviously refers to Nissam Taleb's book *The Black Swan: The Impact of the Highly Improbable.*

Financial Management

Q 3.94: How would you go about preparing a 2–3 page analyst report proposing to a client the acquisition of a waste management firm? How would you collect the information necessary for the valuation?

Q 3.95: How would you value a company? (This is a very popular question.)

Q 3.96: Explain what a discount rate is, and how you calculate it for a publicly traded company. What is the WACC? How would you estimate a firm's beta? How would you calculate the required rate of return for equity holders for a company? What would you use for a market risk premium? How would you estimate the cost of debt for a company (assume that there is no publicly traded debt for that company outstanding)?

Q 3.97: What exactly is a beta and what does it measure? What is systematic risk and how does it differ from active risk?

Q 3.98: Compare the betas of an airport and a retailer.[3]

---

[3] Mullins (1982) has a lovely table in it that lists betas by industry, ranging from Air Transport (1.80) down to Gold (0.35). The article pre-dates the Fama-French critique of the CAPM by 10 years (Fama and French, 1992, 1993) but gives excellent intuition for the CAPM. Watch out for the use of a riskless rate of 10% per annum and an expected return on the market of 19% per annum—which reflect the time period it was written in.

Q 3.99: If you were asked to put together a two-page analyst report on a company, what sort of information would you include? What specific ratios would you include?

Q 3.100: Suppose that the S&P500 index has a P/E ratio of 20. How would you value a manufacturing company with earnings of one million dollars?

Q 3.101: What key financial ratios do you look at when trying to determine a firm's financial health from its balance sheet?

Q 3.102: Why do pharmaceutical companies increase drug prices when they come off patent protection?

Q 3.103: Describe the CAPM.

Q 3.104: Can a company function without working capital?

Q 3.105: What happens to a company's balance sheet if the company buys an asset? Walk me through the steps.

Q 3.106: How would you market this financial product (e.g., a structured note)?

Q 3.107: How do you use DCF to value a skyscraper in order to sell it? You need to come up with current revenue, costs, net income, estimates of future cash flows, and a discount rate.

Q 3.108: Kirk Kekorian attempted to force Chrysler to rid itself of what he called "excess cash"—through higher dividends and a stock buy back. What do you think of this?

Q 3.109: How would you market this company to our clients?

Q 3.110: Have you ever had to fire someone? If so, how did you handle this situation?

Q 3.111: Forecast the income statement for Duracell for this year.

Q 3.112: How do you calculate VaR (i.e., Value at Risk)?

Q 3.113: Have you heard of LTCM?

Q 3.114: What is the difference between default risk and prepayment risk?

Q 3.115: What is kurtosis?

Appendix A

Answers to Brain Teasers

This appendix contains answers to the questions posed in Chapter 1.

A 1.1: This question has appeared over and over again. Although simple, it is rarely answered well. No calculation is required to determine the answer. If you used *any* algebra whatsoever, stop now, go back, reread the question, and try again.

When the quantity Q of water is poured into the alcohol jug, the concentration of alcohol in the alcohol jug becomes $\frac{V}{V+Q}$. After mixing and pouring some back, the concentration of alcohol in the alcohol jug does not change again (because no new water is added). However, when the diluted alcohol is poured back into the water jug, the concentration of water in the water jug changes from 100% to $\frac{V}{V+Q}$. That is, the final concentrations are identical.

How do you see that the final concentrations must be identical? Remember, you do not need any calculations at all. In fact, the only reason for any calculation is if you also want to find out what the final concentrations are (you were not asked this, but if you wish to work it out, your calculations need not go beyond those of the previous paragraph).

Here is how it works. At the end of the process, both jugs contain the same volume of fluid as they did at the start. The only way for the concentration of alcohol (for example) to have changed from 100% is if some alcohol was displaced by water. Similarly, the only way for the concentration of water to have changed from 100% is if some water was displaced by alcohol. Volume is conserved (both total volume and volume in each jug), so all that has happened is that identical quantities of water and alcohol have traded places (and these identical quantities are slightly less than Q). By symmetry, the concentrations of alcohol in the alcohol jug and water in the water jug must be identical.

If you are still stuck, here is another way of thinking about it. Imagine a black bucket with 1,000 black marbles in it and a white bucket with 1,000 white marbles in it. Suppose I take 100 black marbles out of the black bucket and put them in the white bucket and mix it up really well. Then I have 1,100 marbles in the white bucket, and the great majority of them are white. Suppose I then take 100 marbles from those 1,100 and use them to top the black bucket back up to 1,000 marbles. Then both buckets have 1,000 marbles again. Let us suppose that 91 (i.e., the great majority) of the 100 marbles used to top up the black bucket were white. That means I must have returned only 9 of the original 100 black marbles back to the black bucket when I topped it up. That means I must have left 91 black marbles behind in the white bucket—the same as the number of white marbles that migrated over to the black bucket. So, the proportions are identical!

A 1.2:   This is an old favorite. I have tried this out on people and have received almost all imaginable responses. The answer is three, and it cannot be anything else. Two socks can be different, but a third must match one of the first two—giving a matching pair.

A 1.3:   After 100 seconds you can be sure that the ants have all walked off the ruler. The answer is the same as if the ants had perfect vision. The key is that if two ants who collide, immediately about face and continue, then each member of any colliding pair effectively exchanges its exit route with the other; the ants are fungible. It is just as if one of the colliding pair crawled over the other and they both kept going without pause.

A 1.4:   Here are two answers.[1]

1. Turn Switch #1 on. Wait a while. Then turn it off while simultaneously turning Switch #2 on. Go into the room. The illuminated light corresponds to Switch #2. The warm non-illuminated bulb corresponds to Switch #1. The cold non-illuminated bulb corresponds to Switch #3.

2. Guess. You have a one-in-six chance if they are random. However, light switches are not usually random. If you assume the switches are physically located in an order that relates to the physical placement of the bulbs (as they usually are), then you have a fifty-fifty chance!

A 1.5:   First of all, "very small" is classic physics slang for very, very small (i.e., so small that it is a pinpoint mass). If the rock is tossed overboard, the water level falls as though water equal in mass to the mass of the rock is being sucked out of the pool. The rock forces the boat to displace the rock's mass of water. After the rock is gone, the boat rises up, and the water level falls down (Archimedes' Principle).[2]

The next time you are washing dishes, try this experiment. With the sink half-full of water, float a drinking

---

[1] I thank Dahn Tamir for assistance on this question. I am responsible for any errors.

[2] Archimedes said simply that an object in a fluid experiences an upwards force equal to the weight of the fluid that is displaced by the object.

glass. Now drop a steel ball bearing gently into the glass. The glass sinks down, displacing a mass of water equal in mass to the mass of the ball bearing, and the water level rises. Now pluck the ball bearing from the glass, using a magnet. The reverse happens, the glass rises, and the water level falls as though water equal in mass to the mass of the ball bearing is being sucked out of the sink.

Story: There is the old story of the candidate who flew to London for an interview. At the interview, the interviewer excused himself for a few minutes. However, before leaving he asked the interviewee to open a window. Once alone, the interviewee discovered that all the windows were sealed shut. Great! Michael Lewis (in his excellent book Liar's Poker) talks about this technique in use on Wall Street (Lewis, 1990, p27). He suggests that one desperate interviewee threw a chair through Lehman's 43rd floor window in Manhattan!

A 1.6: Let me begin with a "hammer-and-tongs" approach using algebra. When you see how neat the solution is, try to come up with an argument that uses no mathematics whatsoever (I present such an argument after the hammer-and-tongs approach). Please see Figure A.1.

FIRST SOLUTION
Identify the squares using horizontal and vertical indices, counting from the northwest corner. Let i count

down and j count across. Then it is readily seen that the square with coordinates (i, j) has $(i + j - 1)$ cubes on it. It follows that the total number of cubes is given by (in the general case of an $n \times n$ chessboard)[3]

$$\sum_{i=1}^{n} \sum_{j=1}^{n} (i + j - 1)$$

$$= \sum_{i=1}^{n} \sum_{j=1}^{n} [(i - 1) + j]$$

$$= \sum_{i=1}^{n} \left[n(i - 1) + \frac{n(n + 1)}{2} \right]$$

$$= \left[n \left(\frac{n(n + 1)}{2} - n \right) + n \left(\frac{n(n + 1)}{2} \right) \right]$$

$$= n \left(\frac{n^2 + n - 2n + n^2 + n}{2} \right)$$

$$= n^3.$$

The answer n^3 is extremely neat and tidy. In the special case where $n = 20$, there are $20^3 = 8,000$ cubes on the board.

SECOND SOLUTION

With an answer this neat, there must be a non-algebraic solution. Imagine the 20×20 chessboard in front of you, with the stacks of cubes on it as in Figure A.1. Now slice through the cubes horizontally at height 20

---

[3]I make use of the property that $\sum_{j=1}^{n} j = \frac{n(n+1)}{2}$.

units. The cubes above the slice all lie in the southeast lower-triangular section below the non-leading diagonal. Now flip the above-the-slice cubes across the diagonal from southeast to northwest. They will fill the lower stacks to a height of 20 units. You now have a solid cube, and the result follows immediately.

1	2	3	4	$\cdots$	19	20
2	3	4	5	$\cdots$	20	21
3	4	5	6	$\cdots$	21	22
4	5	6	7	$\cdots$	22	23
$\vdots$	$\vdots$	$\vdots$	$\vdots$	$\ddots$	$\vdots$	$\vdots$
19	20	21	22	$\cdots$	37	38
20	21	22	23	$\cdots$	38	39

Figure A.1: Number of Cubes on Each Square of a 20×20 Chessboard (A)

Note: The figure shows the number of cubes on each square of a chessboard, starting with one in the northwest corner and stepping up one each time you step south or east.

Story: Years ago I knew a well-qualified MIT student who got a job offer of \$X from a good firm (a good offer then). He declined, telling them that they had misjudged him. They called him back a couple of days later and offered him \$X × 1.67 instead!

A 1.7: No, definitely not. You cannot tile those 62 squares with the dominoes. If you cannot see why, then go back and think again. This one is too good to waste by peeking at the answers—stop reading here and try again before reading further.

Each domino covers two squares that are side-by-side on the board. Each of these pairs of squares consists of a black and a white. As you place the dominoes, you cover the same number of black squares as white ones. However, the two squares that are off limits are the same color (opposing corners on a chessboard must be the same color). Thus, the number of white squares to be covered is not the same as the number of black, and the dominoes cannot cover them all.[4]

Naoki Sato has supplied an answer to his follow up question. Imagine a closed path on the chessboard that passes through every square exactly once (moving horizontally and vertically, eventually returning to the original square). The two "X"s, unless adjacent, divide

---

[4]An alternative solution has been suggested to me by Aidong Chen. Let each square on the board be described by its coordinates (x, y) for $1 \leq x, y \leq 8$. Any domino covers two adjacent squares, either (x, y) and $(x, y + 1)$, or (x, y) and $(x + 1, y)$. If we add those coordinates up, we get $2x + 2y + 1$ in either case. To tile the 62 remaining squares requires 31 dominoes. If we add up 31 coordinate sums, each of form $2x + 2y + 1$, we must get an odd number. If we add up the coordinate sums of the 62 remaining squares, however, we must get an even number (because the sum of the coordinate sums of all 64 squares is even by symmetry, and the two corners to subtract, (1,1) and (8,8), have even sums). So, it cannot be done.

this path into two sections. Since one "X" is on black, and one is on white, the two sections each cover an even number of squares. They may thus be tiled using the dominoes. If the two "X"s are adjacent, the solution is obvious.

A 1.8:   What is going to happen if you light both ends simultaneously? The two fizzing sparking flames are going to burn toward each other and meet. When they meet 60 seconds worth of fuse has been burnt in two sections that each took the same amount of time. How much time? It has to be exactly 30 seconds because they both took the same time, and these times add to 60 seconds. Of course, you have to bend the fuse so that you can light both ends simultaneously and when they meet it probably won't be in the center of the fuse.

A 1.9:   Light Fuse 1 at both ends and simultaneously light Fuse 2 at one end. As soon as Fuse 1 is burned out (i.e., after 30 seconds), light the other end of Fuse 2.

A 1.10:   If your answer is "none" or "one," then go back and think again. There are, in fact, an uncountably infinite number of starting points that solve this problem.

First of all, you could start at the north pole. On the middle leg of your walk you would always be one mile south of the north pole, so the final leg would put you back where you started. Second, if you start at a point close to the south pole but one mile north of

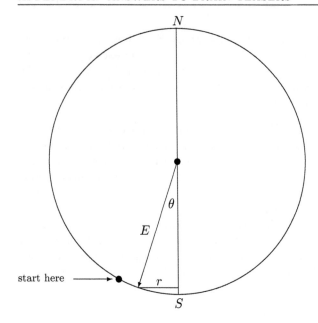

Figure A.2: S-E-N Problem: The Earth

Note: The Earth is a perfect sphere with radius E. You start your trek one mile north of a line of latitude having circumference $1/n$ miles, and radius r miles (so $2\pi r = 1/n$). You must start a distance of $1 + E \cdot \arcsin \frac{1}{2\pi n E}$ miles from the south pole—see Answer 1.10.

a line of latitude having circumference one mile, then the middle leg of your walk begins and ends in the same spot; the final leg takes you back to your starting point (see Figure A.2). There are infinitely many such starting points on the line of latitude that is one mile north of the line of latitude having circumference one mile.

Similarly, if you start slightly further south, at a point one mile north of a line of latitude having circumference one-half mile, then the middle leg of your walk begins and ends in the same spot, and the final leg returns you to your starting point.

More generally, if you begin on a line of latitude one mile north of a line of latitude having circumference $1/n$ miles, then you will walk one mile south, circle the line of latitude n times, and return to your starting point.

In the latter case, how far is your starting point from the south pole? Well, assume the Earth is perfectly spherical, and let E be its radius. Let r be the radius of the line of latitude having circumference $1/n$ miles, so, $2\pi r = 1/n$. A simple sketch shows that the angle θ between the axis of the Earth, and a line drawn from the centre of the Earth to any point on the line of latitude having circumference $1/n$ miles, satisfies $\sin\theta = r/E$ (see Figure A.2). Thus, the arc length from the pole to this line of latitude is the fraction $\frac{\arcsin\frac{r}{E}}{2\pi}$ of the circumference of the Earth, $2\pi E$. That is, the arc length is $E\cdot\arcsin\frac{1}{2\pi nE}$ (using $r = 1/(2\pi n)$). You start one mile north of this, at a distance of $1 + E \cdot \arcsin\frac{1}{2\pi nE}$ miles from the south pole.

A 1.11:   The king should take one coin from bag one, two coins from bag two, three coins from bag three, and so on, finishing with ten coins from bag ten. Place this collection on the weighing device, and look for the discrepancy from $\sum_{i=1}^{10} i$ ounces. If the actual weight is 0.40 ounces short, for example, then bag four is light, and collector four is the cheat.

A 1.12:   Snap the bar into pieces that are one, two, and four parts long, respectively. On day one, give him one part. On day two, exchange your two parts for his one. On day three, give him back the one part. On day four, exchange four parts for his three. On day five, give him one more part. On day six, exchange your two parts for his one. On day seven, give him back the one part.

A 1.13:   Let us attack the mirror problem in stages.

Your Perspective, No Rotations: Put your wristwatch on your left wrist and stand facing a mirror with your arms held out as though you are being crucified (it is a tough interview remember). Your reflected self's wristwatch-bearing arm is pointing the *same* direction as yours. Your wristwatch is to the left of your head, and your reflected self's wristwatch is also to *your* left of his or her head. *There has been no flipping of left for right.* Similarly, if your head is pointing up, then your reflected self's head is also pointing up, and *there has been no flipping of up for down.*

Perhaps this is clearer if you write a sentence on a

transparent plastic sheet, and hold the sheet in front of your body, as though there is no mirror at all and you are simply reading what you have just written. Now look in the mirror. The reflection of your sheet in the mirror is *not* reversed. That is, the left-most word is still left most, the right-most word is still right most, and you can still read the reflected image from left to right.

Viewed from your perspective, everything about you that is left, right, up, or down is still left, right, up, or down, respectively, in your reflected image. There is thus *no* flipping of left for right or up for down. What *has* flipped is that if you are facing east, then your reflection is facing west. It does not matter for the sentence written on the transparent sheet, because it has no depth. It does matter for you, because your reflected nose is facing the opposite direction.

Your Perspective, Rotation of Yourself: If your interviewer suggests that there really is a flipping left for right of your reflected self, but not up for down, then this requires an implicit rotation of your perspective about a vertical axis, to place your right-handed self into the imagined boots of your reflected self who is left handed and standing on the other side of the mirror. To get a one-to-one mapping (so the boots fit), however, you still need to flip yourself left for right (without changing the direction in which you are facing) because your wristwatch is on your left wrist—the opposite of your reflected self. Had you instead

49

APPENDIX A. ANSWERS TO BRAIN TEASERS

rotated yourself about a horizontal axis, and then attempted to place yourself into the imagined boots of your reflected self, you would find your noses pointing the same direction and your wristwatches on the same sides, but your head would be between the feet of your reflected self, and to get into those imagined boots, you would still need to flip yourself up for down (without changing the direction in which you are facing).

The fact that neither a rotation about a horizontal nor a vertical axis suffices to place you into the imagined boots of your reflected self, confirms my earlier assertion: There is no flipping of left for right, nor up for down, but rather, a flipping in the direction of the depth. If your interviewer firmly believes that a mirror does flip left for right, then he or she is predisposed toward rotation about a vertical axis (something many of us do every day), and has not thought through the consequences of the attempted one-to-one mapping.

A 1.14: Yes, it can be done, in theory if not in practice. If you are stuck and looking for a hint, think about inverting a condom and covering it with another.

Let us label the condoms $C1$, and $C2$, and the men $M1$, $M2$, and $M3$. $M1$ wears $C1$ with $C2$ placed over it. $M2$ then uses $C2$, which is still clean inside. $M3$ then wears $C1$ inverted ($C1$'s outside, you will recall, was kept clean by $C2$), and places the twice-used $C2$ over it. Don't try this at home.

A 1.15: No, of course not. Replace the word "prime"

with any other word, and the answer is still no. If they are consecutive, then by definition there are none of them in between!

A 1.16: People are fed by the area, A, of the pizza. $A = \pi r^2 = \pi \left(\frac{d}{2}\right)^2 = \frac{\pi}{4}d^2$, where d is the diameter. Thus, $d = \sqrt{\frac{4}{\pi}}\sqrt{A}$. Multiplying A by $\frac{8}{6}$ requires a multiplicative change of $\sqrt{\frac{8}{6}}$ in d. That is, $d' = \sqrt{\frac{8}{6}}d = 13.86$ inches. Without a calculator, the square root of $(1 + X)$ is roughly $(1 + \frac{X}{2})$, so $\sqrt{\frac{8}{6}} \approx \sqrt{1.33} \approx 1.15$. Fifteen percent of 12 is 1.8, so the answer is roughly 13.8 inches.

A derivatives question with the same answer is: A six-month at-the-money call has price \$12; what is the price of the eight-month call? You can answer this using the approximation $c = S\sigma\sqrt{\frac{T-t}{2\pi}}$ (Crack, 2009).

A 1.17: This is a very old problem, and a common interview question. The probability that the first head occurs on toss k is $\left(\frac{1}{2}\right)^k$; this event carries with it a payoff of \$$2^k$. The contribution of toss k to the expected payoff is thus $\left(\frac{1}{2}\right)^k \times \$2^k = \$1$. This is the same for each k. The expected payoff to the game as a whole is the summation over all k of these payoffs. This is $\$1 + \$1 + \$1 + \cdots = \$\infty$. The expected payoff to the game is infinite!

This is called the "St. Petersburg Game." The fact that the expected payoff to the game is infinite, and that no one in his or her right mind would pay more than a few hundred dollars to play, is why it is sometimes called the "St. Petersburg Paradox." There are several ways that you can think about this sensibly.

One way is to note that "value" is not the same thing as "expected payoff";[5] value equals *utility* of expected payoff. Most people cannot distinguish between very large amounts of money.[6] This means that 2^{50} is not worth twice 2^{49}. However, these very large amounts are counted in exactly this way when calculating expected payoff to the game as a whole. If you think that $2^k = \$2^{50}$ (essentially) for all $k \geq 50$, then the expected payoff to the game is finite:

$$\$50 + \$2^{50} \times \left(\frac{1}{2^{51}} + \frac{1}{2^{52}} + \frac{1}{2^{53}} + \dots \right) = \$51$$

A spread could be quoted around this, maybe ($10, $200). How much would you pay your customer to play? How much would you charge your customer?

A second way to think about this is in terms of default risk.[7] We need to quote the bid (what we pay) and the ask (what the customer pays). For the bid, it is the customer's default risk we need to worry about.

---

[5]It is important to note that the Weak Law of Large Numbers fails if the expectation is not finite (Feller, 1968, pp251).

[6]Bernoulli (1738; 1954) suggests that utility of payoffs should depend upon how wealthy you are. For a practitioner's view of utility, see Kritzman (1992).

[7]I thank Olivier Ledoit for suggesting this solution technique. I am responsible for any errors.

Let us assume a wealthy customer who defaults above one million dollars. In this case, the customer defaults after (about) 20 tosses. Assuming the investment bank is of large scale, a payoff from the customer between two dollars and one million dollars is of relatively small size. The investment bank takes such bets every day, and this one is uncorrelated with all the others. At this level, we could argue that the investment bank is risk-neutral and so the bid is exactly \$20 with no risk premium.

For the ask, it is the company that risks bankruptcy and default. Let us assume that the company files for bankruptcy after losing one billion dollars (on the order of magnitude of Barings, and Metallgesellschaft)—approximately $\$2^{30}$. The expected value of the game to the customer is thus about \$30—the bank defaults after 30 tosses. However, your career and the holdings of all the shareholders can be destroyed by this bet, so you had better add a considerable risk premium. You might want to go all the way up to \$200 and quote a bid-ask of (\$20, \$200)—it depends upon your degree of risk aversion.

Each of these two solutions uses a truncation method. Another method is to think about feasibility. If it does take more than 50 tosses to get a head, then the payoff is not feasible because $\$2^{50}$ is more dollars than there are atoms in the universe, and whoever sold the ticket to the game is—by the laws of physics—unable to pay. See also Feller (1968, pp251–253).

A 1.18: I give an elegant answer first, and then a hammer-and-tongs one that could be useful for variations of the game.

FIRST SOLUTION

The original game is stated as "You toss five coins and I toss four coins. You win if you get strictly more heads." This game is isomorphic to an analytically simpler game.[8] "You toss four coins and I toss four coins. Whomever gets the most heads wins immediately. If we are tied, however, then you toss one more coin to decide the outcome." By observation, both stages of this second game are completely symmetric. So, we each have a probability one half of winning.

SECOND SOLUTION

A simple sketch of the joint density of our outcomes, and an appeal to symmetry, gives the answer as $1/2$ without any calculation. I derive the answer graphically, with more details than you need.

The key to this more complex solution is to recognize that when $p = 1/2$, the binomial density $B(N, p)$ that counts the number of heads of either player is symmetric, and that two people tossing coins independently of each other means that the joint density is just the product of the marginals.[9]

---

[8] I thank Tommaso Sechi for suggesting this elegant approach.

[9] The binomial distribution $B(N, p)$ has skewness $\frac{q-p}{\sqrt{Npq}}$ and kurtosis $3 - \frac{6}{N} + \frac{1}{Npq}$; these go to zero and three, respectively, as $N \to \infty$ (i.e., the distribution converges to normality). See Evans et al. (1993) for more details.

To make the intuition clear, I will consider first the simpler case where you toss only two coins and I toss only one. I give all the fine details to make it clear, which may be useful in variations of the game, but in fact, no calculation is needed. Each toss is a Bernoulli trial with probability of success (i.e., a head) equal to $1/2$. The tosses are independent, so the count of heads Y that you get is distributed binomial: $f_Y(y) = P(Y = y) = \binom{N}{y} p^y q^{N-y}$, where $N = 2$, $p = \frac{1}{2}$, $q \equiv 1 - p = \frac{1}{2}$. So, $f_Y(y) = \binom{2}{y} \left(\frac{1}{2}\right)^y \left(\frac{1}{2}\right)^{2-y} = \binom{2}{y} \left(\frac{1}{2}\right)^2$. Similarly, with X as the number of heads in one toss of a fair coin, $P(X = x) = f_X(x) = \binom{1}{x} \left(\frac{1}{2}\right)^1$. The marginals are thus given by

$$
f_Y(y) = \begin{cases} \frac{1}{4}, & y = 0, \\ \frac{1}{2}, & y = 1, \\ \frac{1}{4}, & y = 2, \end{cases} \quad \text{and} \quad f_X(x) = \begin{cases} \frac{1}{2}, & x = 0, \\ \frac{1}{2}, & x = 1. \end{cases}
$$

The random variables Y and X are statistically independent of each other, so the joint density is just the product of the marginals $P(X = x, Y = y) = f_{XY}(x, y) = f_X(x) \cdot f_Y(y)$ as shown in Table A.1. Simple visual inspection of Table A.1 shows that in the simple case of two and one tosses, we get $P(Y > X) = 1/2$ (i.e., the sum of the shaded cells).

Although I gave the formal calculation of the marginal and joint densities in this simplified case, this calculation is not needed. The two marginal Binomial dis-

Table A.1: Binomial Joint Density: Two Tosses versus
One Toss

	$f_{XY}(x,y)$	0 $\left[\frac{1}{4}\right]$	1 $\left[\frac{1}{2}\right]$	2 $\left[\frac{1}{4}\right]$
			$Y\ [f_Y(y)]$	
$X\ [f_X(x)]$	0 $\left[\frac{1}{2}\right]$	$\frac{1}{8}$	$\frac{2}{8}$	$\frac{1}{8}$
	1 $\left[\frac{1}{2}\right]$	$\frac{1}{8}$	$\frac{2}{8}$	$\frac{1}{8}$

Y is the number of heads in two tosses of a fair coin. X is
the number of heads in one toss of a fair coin. The binomial marginal densities $f_X(x)$ and $f_Y(y)$ are shown in square
brackets. The tosses are all independent. So, the binomial
joint density $f_{XY}(x,y)$ is the product of the marginals. The
sum of the shaded cells is $P(Y > X) = 1/2$.

tributions shown in square brackets in Table A.1 are
symmetric because $p = 1/2$. With both marginals
symmetric, it must be that the sum of the joint probabilities in the shaded cells and the sum of the joint
probabilities in the un-shaded cells are the same. The
two sums must add to one, so the sum of the shaded
cells must be $P(Y > X) = 1/2$.

Table A.2 shows an analogous table for the case of
you tossing five coins and me tossing four coins. The
symmetrical marginals mean that the joint density is
symmetric in all respects. If you take a pair of scissors
and cut out the shaded cells as a single inverted stair-

case, then rotate that through 180 degrees, the contents perfectly match the contents of the un-shaded cells. So, by symmetry, $P(Y > X) = 1/2$. I have given all the details of the marginal and joint densities in Table A.2, but in fact, no numbers are required to do the calculation; I have given them only to fill in the fine details to back up the answer.

A 1.19: This has been a very popular question. Assume that neither of you peek into your envelopes. Assume that you have $\$X$ in your envelope, where $\$X$ has a fifty-fifty chance of being either $\$m$ or $\$2m$. This means that your opponent's envelope has a fifty-fifty chance of containing $\$2X$ or $\$\frac{1}{2}X$. The expected value of switching is

$$\left(\frac{1}{2} \times \$2X\right) + \left(\frac{1}{2} \times \$\frac{1}{2}X\right) = \$1.25X.$$

The expected *benefit* of switching is, therefore, $\$0.25X$. On this basis, it looks as though you should switch envelopes. Of course, if your opponent does not peek, and she has $\$Y$ in her envelope, exactly the same argument shows that she has an expected benefit to switching of $\$0.25Y$. So, it looks as though she should switch also. This is the first part of the "Exchange Paradox": it seems that you *both* benefit from switching.

Now, suppose that neither of you peek and that you do switch envelopes once. If you still do not peek, then a repeat of exactly the same argument suggests

Table A.2: Binomial Joint Density: Five Tosses versus Four Tosses

		Y $[f_Y(y)]$					
	$f_{XY}(x,y)$	$0\left[\frac{1}{32}\right]$	$1\left[\frac{5}{32}\right]$	$2\left[\frac{10}{32}\right]$	$3\left[\frac{10}{32}\right]$	$4\left[\frac{5}{32}\right]$	$5\left[\frac{1}{32}\right]$
$X\ [f_X(x)]$	$0\left[\frac{1}{16}\right]$	$\frac{1}{512}$	$\frac{5}{512}$	$\frac{10}{512}$	$\frac{10}{512}$	$\frac{5}{512}$	$\frac{1}{512}$
	$1\left[\frac{4}{16}\right]$	$\frac{4}{512}$	$\frac{20}{512}$	$\frac{40}{512}$	$\frac{40}{512}$	$\frac{20}{512}$	$\frac{4}{512}$
	$2\left[\frac{6}{16}\right]$	$\frac{6}{512}$	$\frac{30}{512}$	$\frac{60}{512}$	$\frac{60}{512}$	$\frac{30}{512}$	$\frac{6}{512}$
	$3\left[\frac{4}{16}\right]$	$\frac{4}{512}$	$\frac{20}{512}$	$\frac{40}{512}$	$\frac{40}{512}$	$\frac{20}{512}$	$\frac{4}{512}$
	$4\left[\frac{1}{16}\right]$	$\frac{1}{512}$	$\frac{5}{512}$	$\frac{10}{512}$	$\frac{10}{512}$	$\frac{5}{512}$	$\frac{1}{512}$

Y is the number of heads in five tosses of a fair coin. X is the number of heads in four tosses of a fair coin. The binomial marginal densities $f_X(x) = \binom{4}{x}\left(\frac{1}{2}\right)^4$ and $f_Y(y) = \binom{5}{y}\left(\frac{1}{2}\right)^5$ are shown in square brackets. The tosses are all independent. So, the binomial joint density $f_{XY}(x,y)$ is the product of the marginals.

an expected benefit of 0.25 of the contents of your envelope if you switch again. The same applies to your opponent. This is the second part of the "Exchange Paradox": it seems that you could happily switch forever (like a dog chasing its own tail). The foregoing is the naive answer.

The problem is twofold: First, you are assuming that value is expected payoff (this is so only if you are genuinely risk-neutral);[10] second, your "prior" beliefs are that you have a fifty-fifty chance of having either m or $2m$. The first problem is a function of your individual risk preferences and is difficult to address. The second problem can be tackled using two approaches: the first approach is to reconsider the nature of your prior; the second approach is to "update" your prior probability assessment (this is "Bayesian" statistics as opposed to "classical" statistics).

The first approach is to reconsider the nature of your priors. Our previous (paradoxical) calculation yielded

---

[10] An aside is in order. In corporate finance, the present value of a projected random payout is the discounted expected cash flow. The discounting is done at a rate that incorporates risk (e.g., using the CAPM), and the expectation is a mathematical one using real world probabilities (Brealey and Myers, 1991). An alternative to the real world expected cash flow coupled with the risk-adjusted discount rate is a risk-neutral world expected cash flow coupled with a riskless discount rate. The former is popular in corporate finance; the latter is popular in option pricing (see Arnold and Crack (2004) and Arnold, Crack and Schwartz (2009, 2010)). With no discounting (e.g., the envelope question), value is expected payoff only if you are risk-neutral.

$1.25X as the expected payoff to switching. However, this assumes that for any given X, it is equally likely that your opponent has $2X or $\frac{1}{2}X$. If you do not peek, then you are assuming a "diffuse level prior" because you assume this equality of likelihood for *any* X. Your prior is, therefore, not a valid probability density function (pdf) because the probabilities—across X— do not sum to **1**. However, for any *particular* m, it is equally likely that you received one of $m or $2m. Thus, for any particular m, your priors are a pdf and any paradoxes should disappear. The expected value of switching should be zero. This is easily demonstrated. Let $P(\$m)$ denote the probability that *you* got $m (the lower amount); let $E(V)$ denote the expected value to switching; then $E(V)$ is given by

$$E(V) = [E(V|\$m) \times P(\$m)] +$$
$$[E(V|\$2m) \times P(\$2m)]$$
$$= \left(+\$m \times \frac{1}{2}\right) + \left(-\$m \times \frac{1}{2}\right)$$
$$= \$0.$$

The expected value is zero, and you are thus indifferent— resolving the paradox.[11] Note that $E(V|\$m) = +\$m$ because, conditional on your having been given the envelope containing only $m, you gain $m by switching.

The second approach is to update your prior. To update your prior, you need information. The most ob-

---

[11]I thank Andres Almazan for suggesting this type of solution technique. I am responsible for any errors.

vious source of information is to peek into your envelope. So, assume that both you and your opponent peek into your envelopes. Now it gets subjective. If you see an amount that *seems* very high, then you update your prior probabilities: the probability that you have the high-value envelope increases, and the probability that you have the low-value envelope decreases. You no longer see value in switching envelopes.[12] If you see an amount that *seems* very low, then you see value in switching. The problem now is that you must subjectively assess the amount in the envelope as being either "low" or "high." The "Bayesian Resolution of the Exchange Paradox" is covered in detail in Christensen and Utts (1992).

If you have both peeked, and you do switch, then you will not switch again. This is because one of you gained, and that person will not want to lose by switching back. A similar question (but with an upper bound on the quantities possible) appears in Dixit and Nalebuff (1991, Chapter 13). The Dixit and Nalebuff book on strategic thinking is well worth a look.

A 1.20: You win with probability 1/3. Wind is effectively absent from the sample space—it does not affect your chances of winning or losing. You lose with probability 1/3 at the first turn. You thus have only a 2/3

---

[12]However, you might argue that if you see an amount that seems so high that even one-half of it is more money than you can comprehend, you might switch envelopes just for the hell of it; it is worth the gamble.

possibility of even getting to turn a second card. If you do get to turn the second card, there is 50% chance that it will be Fire and you lose, and a 50% chance it will not be, and you win. Thus the probability of winning is 50% of 2/3.

Story: Let me give some unorthodox advice. I was given an inexpensive book called *The Dirty Dozen* written by Sergeant Major (Ret.) Lawrence A. Jordan. Sergeant Major Jordan served a 24-year Special Operations career with the U.S. Army Rangers and Special Forces. His book is about dirty fighting techniques, and Chapter 2, *The Winning Mind*, is about mental preparation for life-or-death hand-to-hand combat in self defence. Although it is unorthodox of me to write this, I recommend that you read *The Winning Mind* chapter of *The Dirty Dozen* for interview preparation. If you can stomach it, it may give you just the edge you need.

Appendix B

Answers to Thinking Questions

A 2.1: The "how many somethings are there somewhere" questions are common. There is no precise algebraic solution routine. You make several rough assumptions and hope the errors cancel. For example, the US population is about 300,000,000 (2014). The population of Bloomington, Indiana, is about 100,000 (when the students are there). There are about six McDonald's in Bloomington. I calculate $\frac{300,000,000}{100,000} \times 6 = 3,000 \times 6 = 18,000$. However, Bloomington is a college town, and students eat more junk food than the general populace, so I adjust my answer downwards to about 10,000 to 15,000 McDonald's outlets in the US.

Looking at online profiles of the company, I estimate that of 34,000 McDonalds restaurants (2014), roughly 14,000 of them are located in the US.

In general, you grab something you know, scale it up or down, and adjust for any biases. Let us try it again a different way. I cannot believe anyone over 30 or under five would eat in a McDonald's. If lifespan is uniformly distributed between zero and 75 years, then only one-third of the population (100,000,000) is eligible for eating at McDonald's. Half of these are health nuts. That leaves 50,000,000 customers. Suppose they eat four meals per week. That works out to about 30,000,000 meals served per day. If one outlet sells a burger every 30 seconds, that is 120 an hour and about 3,000 per day. 30,000,000 meals served per day at 3,000 per outlet implies about 10,000 outlets. This is still in the ballpark.

Whether it is ping-pong balls in a 747, barbers in Chicago, or elevators in the US, find something you know and scale it up or down. Be sure to know the population of the Earth, the US, the city you live in, and the city you interview in.

A 2.2: The answer given by the interviewer was that you should threaten to kill yourself by hitting your head against the wall. The administrative nightmare that would follow would ruin the guard's upcoming weekend. He would have to give you a cigarette.

A 2.3: You have to figure that the coin is not fair.

The probability of another head is essentially one. See Huff's book, "How to Lie with Statistics," for related arguments (Huff, 1982, Chapter 3).

In one of my other books, *Foundations for Scientific Investing* (Crack, 2014), I describe an experiment I performed in an undergraduate classroom. A student rolled a pair of dice 36 times and we recorded on how many occasions a 7 or 11 occurred. We then compared the outcome to a Binomial table. Then it was my turn. I palmed the fair dice and swapped them for a loaded pair that always gives me a 7 or 11. As the odds stacked up against me, the students watched in amazement. Even when there was only one chance in a million that what they saw could be the result of rolling fair dice, there were still a few students in a class of over a 100 stubbornly clinging to the belief that the dice were fair. If I did the same in an MBA or PhD class, the wizened students would all see through it immediately, but some undergraduates are amazingly naive.

A 2.4: I have had several comments from readers on how to weigh a jet plane: Land it on an aircraft carrier and measure the displacement of the ship; land it on the ice (e.g., Arctic) and then crash into it with something big and see how far it moves; look at the size of the tire footprints and deduce it from the tire pressure. How about just looking in the manual?

A 2.5: I spent some time at NASA's web site. NASA says there are four forces on an aeroplane: thrust, drag, weight and lift. These forces move the aeroplane forward, backward, downward, and upward, respectively, and simultaneously. For example, level forward flight would require that lift balance weight, and that thrust more than compensate for drag.

NASA indicates that there is considerable debate and confusion over how lift is generated. They describe lift as a mechanical force that is generated when a solid object moves through a fluid and "turns" the fluid flow. The shape and "angle of attack" of an aeroplane's wing turn the fluid flow downwards, and, by Newton's Third Law of Motion (i.e., for every action there is an equal and opposite reaction) this provides upward lift.

NASA comments that wings are often shaped so that the wing, taken in cross section, has more surface area on the top surface than the bottom surface. The air flows more quickly over the top of the wing than the bottom. The variation in velocity of the fluid creates a pressure differential that produces lift. They state, however, that this wing shape is not necessary to create lift. Rather, it only contributes to it.

A 2.6:   A "tombstone" is an advertisement that lists (like the names on a tombstone) the underwriters associated with a public issue of a security. The particular placement of the underwriters' names on the tombstone carries with it implications for the perceived status of the underwriters on the deal.

A student came to see me. He told me that he was flying to Chicago the next day for a job interview with an investment bank. He asked me what sort of non-quantitative questions he might face, so I pulled out my book and tried several on him. When I got to the tombstone question, I stopped and asked him if he knew the definition of a tombstone. I pulled out that day's *Wall Street Journal* (WSJ) to see if there was a tombstone in the third section. The page at which I opened the WSJ contained a tombstone from the bank he was going to interview with the next day! I clipped it out and gave it to him, and he talked about it in his interview.

A 2.7: This is not necessarily a rejection. It may just be a test to see how you defend yourself. It is just the opposite way of asking you why you fit the job. A colleague of mine told me that he once started an interview with the statement "I don't think you are the right person for the job." He believed it, but he knew the candidate was talented, and he was interviewing him just in case. My colleague thought the candidate would tell him why he was the right person, but instead the candidate just deflated like a tire with a slow leak. The interview was a complete bust. If someone said that to me, I would answer "No! I fit because ..."

A 2.8: Popping a balloon. Playing the drums on my desk. Stabbing it in the eye of an attacking shark. Doodling (that's not writing). Moving it across my desk one inch at a time to count how many interview candidates I have rejected this week. As a straight edge for drawing a diagram with a pen. Centering something that I am about to screw to a piece of wood (by gripping the pencil with thumb and forefinger to measure the distance from one edge, and then moving the gripped pencil to the other side for comparison). Conducting music. As a splint when I break my finger. As kindling to start a fire. Creating pencil shavings with a pencil sharpener.

Story: I was telephone-interviewing a candidate for an active equity research job in London. His job would be the creation, testing, and implementation of strategies for beating the market. I asked him if he could draw upon his considerable experience in the markets to suggest to me a strategy he had heard of for beating the market. There was a very long pause (at least 20 seconds, which is a long time to hear nothing down a phone line), after which he answered simply "no." What did he think I was going to ask him about?!

A 2.9:   Asking about market efficiency is very common in portfolio management interviews. Market efficiency means that prices (typically stock prices) reflect information to the extent that consistent positive trading profits cannot be made after accounting for transaction costs, taxes and risk aversion (each of which retards trading on news). There is a great deal of empirical evidence over the last 50 years to suggest that markets are largely efficient. Nevertheless, there exist many small deviations from efficiency, even in the larger markets, and prices that respond to news correctly *on average* (which is what most academic studies look at) leave much room for under- and over-reaction, and for trading opportunities.

A 2.10: The "Dow Jones Dogs strategy" involves buying the "Dow Jones Dogs" at the start of the year. These are the 10 Dow Jones Industrial Average (DJIA) stocks with the highest dividend yield. They are dogs because you get a relatively high dividend yield by having a low price relative to dividends. You are supposed to rebalance the portfolio every year. Historically this has been a profitable strategy. The CBOE introduced options on a Dow Jones Dogs index (ticker symbol "MUT") in 1999, but I do not see any evidence of them in 2014. Deutsche Bank offers an exchange-traded note (ETN) based on the return to the Dow Jones Dogs strategy (ticker symbol "DOD"). MUT and DOD move very closely together.

A 2.11: This is basic macroeconomics, and you should be fully familiar with it. The two forms of macroeconomic policy are monetary policy and fiscal policy. Monetary policy tries to achieve the broad objectives of economic policy through control of the monetary system and by operating on the supply of money, the level and structure of interest rates, and other conditions affecting the supply of credit (Pearce, 1984, p291). With monetary policy, the Federal Reserve Bank ("the Fed") sell bonds and reduces the money supply—an "open market operation." This increases interest rates (the cost of money) and makes capital expenditures more costly. This in turn slows down growth in the economy and should fight the inflationary threat.

In addition to open market operations, the Fed implements monetary policy by managing the discount rate (the rate the Fed charges banks for loans), adjusting the Fed funds rate (the rate banks charge each other for loans of federal funds), managing reserve requirements for banks (the proportion of a bank's assets required to be held in Treasury securities), and operations in the government repo (i.e., repurchase) market.[1]

Fiscal policy refers to the use of taxation and government expenditure to regulate the aggregate level of economic activity (Pearce, 1984, p160). Increasing taxes and decreasing government spending should slow down growth in the economy and fight inflationary fears. Go to any standard macroeconomic text if you want more details on fiscal or monetary policy.

A 2.12: The answer given by the interviewer was that if you are Avis or Hertz, cars are inventory. The same

---

[1] A "repo" is a repurchase agreement. It is an agreement to repurchase a security in the future. You give up the security now in exchange for cash, agreeing to repurchase the security at a later date for a larger amount of cash. A repo is thus a collateralized loan. A reverse repo is the other side of the deal—you purchase securities now with an agreement to sell them later. Repos range in maturity from overnight ("O/N") to as long as five years; shorter-term repos are the most popular.

applies to an automobile manufacturer (or any of their distributors).

A 2.13:   From memory, the Empire State Building is about 100 floors high. Looking at the building I am sitting in, I figure each floor is about four meters high. A roll of quarters costs $10, so it must have 40 quarters in it. It is about three inches long. There are 39 inches in a meter. So, I need $100 \times 4 \times 39 \div 3$ rolls of quarters. That is $100 \times 4 \times 13$ rolls of quarters each with 40 quarters. So, that is $5,200 \times 40$ quarters. That is 208,000 quarters.

A 2.14:   No. FCF does not include interest payments or repayment of principal because FCF is the cash flows generated by net assets and available to the owners of the company (both debt and equity holders). The tax benefit of interest payments is recognized in a lower after tax cost of debt in the WACC. Finally, financing costs are not cash outflows. They do not reduce cash available to owners. To the contrary, they *are* cash payments to owners and, therefore, have no net effect on cash flows available to owners (i.e., FCF).

A 2.15:   Tapered cans are stronger, for the same reason that car doors often have a curve in them. Tapered cans can be stacked (assuming the tapered bottom just fits within the tapered top). A tapered can uses less material in the lid.

A 2.16:   You can knock two zeros of the argument of $\sqrt{204,000}$ and add one to the answer. So $\sqrt{204,000} =$

$10 \times \sqrt{2,040} = 100 \times \sqrt{20.4}$. Now you just need to estimate $\sqrt{20.4}$. Well, 4 is too small, and 5 is too big, and 20 is roughly half way between 16 and 25. So, I will guess 4.5 (times 100). Do not assume that because the argument starts with a 2, that its square root starts with $\sqrt{2} \approx 1.4142$, because that logic works only if the 2 is followed by an even number of zeros.

A 2.17: There are several possible responses that make sense. An obvious reason is safety: a round cover cannot fall down a round hole. Whereas if both hole and cover are either square or rectangular or oval, the cover can easily fall down the hole if lifted vertically and turned diagonally and dropped. Incidentally, I noticed while working in New Zealand that some of their manholes have rectangular covers. However, in this case, the covers are hinged and attached to a frame that is immovable—thus preventing the cover from falling.

Another reason for being round is that the (very heavy) covers may be rolled easily. Similarly, a (very heavy) round cover need not be manipulated before being returned to its hole—it may be replaced in any orientation. Finally, and with some sarcasm, manhole covers are round because the holes that they cover are round. It is easier to drill a round hole in the street than a square one. Have you ever tried drilling a *square* hole in anything?

References

Arnold, Tom, and Timothy Falcon Crack, 2004, "Using the WACC to Value Real Options," *Financial Analysts Journal*, Vol 60 No 6, (November/December), pp78–82.

Arnold, Tom, Timothy Falcon Crack, and Adam Schwartz, 2009, "Inferring Risk-Averse Probability Distributions from Options Prices Using Implied Binomial Trees: Additional Theory, Empirics, and Extensions." Working paper. Available at SSRN: http://ssrn.com/abstract=749904.

Arnold, Tom, Timothy Falcon Crack, and Adam Schwartz, 2010 "Inferring Risk-Averse Probability Distributions from Options Prices Using Implied Binomial Trees." A chapter in: G.N. Gregoriou and R. Pascalau (Eds.), Financial Econometrics Handbook. Chapman-Hall-CRC/Taylor and Francis: London, UK.

Bernoulli, Daniel, 1738, "Speciman Theoriae Novae de Mensura Sortis," *Papers of the Imperial Academy of Sciences in Petersburg*, Vol V, pp175–192. Note that an English Translation appears in Bernoulli (1954).

Bernoulli, Daniel, 1954, "Exposition of a New Theory on the Measurement of Risk," *Econometrica*, Vol 22 No 1, (January), pp23–36 (Translated from the Latin by Louise Sommer).

Brealey, Richard A. and Stewart C. Myers, 1991, *Principles of Corporate Finance*, Fourth Edition, McGraw-Hill: New York, NY.

Christensen, Ronald and Jessica Utts, 1992, "Bayesian Resolution of the 'Exchange Paradox'," *The American Statistician*, Vol 46 No 4, (November), pp274–276.

Crack, Timothy Falcon, 2004, *Basic Black-Scholes: Option Pricing and Trading*. See www.BasicBlackScholes.com, and the advertisement on the second to last page of this book, for details.

Crack, Timothy Falcon, 2009, *Basic Black-Scholes: Option Pricing and Trading*. Revised Second Edition. See www.BasicBlackScholes.com, and the advertisement on the second to last page of this book, for details.

Crack, Timothy Falcon, 2014, Foundations for Scientific Investing: Capital Markets Intuition and Critical Thinking Skills, See www.FoundationsForScientificInvesting.com, and the advertisement on the last page of this book, for details.

Derman, Emanuel, 2004, *My Life as a Quant: Reflections on Physics and Finance*, Wiley: Hoboken, NJ.

Dixit, Avinash K. and Barry J. Nalebuff, 1991, *Thinking Strategically: The Competitive Edge in Business, Politics, and Everyday Life*, Norton: New York, NY.

74

Evans, Merran, Nicholas Hastings, and Brian Peacock, 1993, *Statistical Distributions*, Second Edition, John Wiley and Sons: New York, NY.

Fama, Eugene F. and Kenneth R. French, 1992, "The Cross-Section of Expected Stock Returns," *The Journal of Finance*, Vol 47 No 2, (June), pp427–465.

Fama, Eugene F. and Kenneth R. French, 1993, "Common Risk Factors in the Returns on Stocks and Bonds," *Journal of Financial Economics*, Vol. 33 No. 1, (February), pp3–56.

Feller, William, 1968, *An Introduction to Probability Theory and its Applications*, Volume I, Third Edition, John Wiley and Sons: New York, NY.

Huff, Darrell, 1982, *How to Lie with Statistics*, Norton: New York, NY.

Kritzman, Mark, 1992, "What Practitioners Need to Know About Utility," *The Financial Analysts Journal*, Vol 48 No 3, (May/June), pp17–20.

Lewis, Michael M., 1990, *Liar's Poker: Rising Through the Wreckage of Wall Street*, Penguin Books: New York, NY.

Mullins, David W., 1982, "Does the Capital Asset Pricing Model Work?," *Harvard Business Review*, Vol 60 No 1, (January/February), pp105–114.

REFERENCES

Index

Basic Black-Scholes:
Option Pricing and Trading

Timothy Falcon Crack

BSc (HONS 1st Class), PGDipCom, MCom, PhD (MIT), IMC

Extremely clear explanations of Black-Scholes option pricing theory, and applications of the theory to option trading. The presentation does not go far beyond basic Black-Scholes because a novice need not go far beyond Black-Scholes to make money in the options markets, all high-level option pricing theory is simply an extension of Black-Scholes, there already exist many books that look far beyond Black-Scholes without first laying the firm foundation given here. The second edition includes Bloomberg screens, expanded analysis of Black-Scholes interpretations, and is accompanied by two downloadable spreadsheets (to forecast profits and transactions costs to option positions, and to explore option sensitivities including the Greeks).

www.BasicBlackScholes.com
timcrack@alum.mit.edu

Foundations for Scientific Investing: Capital Markets Intuition and Critical Thinking Skills

Timothy Falcon Crack

BSc (HONS 1st Class), PGDipCom, MCom, PhD (MIT), IMC

This book lays a firm foundation for thinking about and conducting investment. It does this by helping to build capital markets intuition and critical thinking skills. Every investor needs these skills to conduct confident, deliberate, and skeptical investment. This book is the product of 25 years of investment experience and 20 painstaking years of destructive testing in university classrooms. Although the topic is applied investments, the integration of finance, economics, accounting, pure mathematics, statistics, numerical techniques, and spreadsheets (or programming) make this an ideal capstone course at the advanced undergraduate or masters/MBA level. The material should be accessible to a motivated practitioner or talented individual investor with only high school level mathematics.

www.FoundationsForScientificInvesting.com
timcrack@alum.mit.edu

Pocket Heard on The Street: Quantitative Questions from Finance Job Interivews

Timothy Falcon Crack

BSc (HONS 1st Class), PGDipCom, MCom, PhD (MIT), IMC

A complement to the pocket edition you are holding. This pocket edition contains a careful selection of 75 of the best quantitative questions collected from actual job interviews in investment banking, investment management, and options trading. The interviewers use the same questions year-after-year, and here they are with solutions!

The questions in these pocket editions are a careful selection from the full sized edition of Heard on The Street: Quantitative Questions from Wall Street Job Interviews. The full size edition is the first and the original book of quantitative questions from finance job interviews. Painstakingly revised over 18 years and 14 editions, it has been shaped by feedback from many hundreds of readers. With over 50,000 copies in print, its readership is unmatched by any competing book.

www.InvestmentBankingJobInterviews.com
timcrack@alum.mit.edu

Milton Keynes UK
Ingram Content Group UK Ltd.
UKHW020750111223
434160UK00016B/826

9 780994 103826